Little Leit
The Importance of being Tiny

Elisabeth Tyndall

Illustrated By Joey Weiser

AuthorHouse™
1663 Liberty Drive
Bloomington, IN 47403
www.authorhouse.com
Phone: 1-800-839-8640

First published by AuthorHouse 10/6/2010

ISBN: 978-1-4520-5363-9 (sc)

Library of Congress Control Number: 2010912800

Printed in the United States of America

This book is printed on acid-free paper.

authorHOUSE®

For Chris

This is a story about a small, tiny leaf, who thought he was not important, and felt very sad because of this. His name was Leif. Leif thought he was not important, because he was not something big and powerful. He was not a big tall tree, or a bright coloured flower. He thought that only the big things in the world got noticed. He believed he was tiny and unimportant. He believed he was a truly insignificant leaf.

When Leif first fell off the tree and the wind blew him around the yard, he said glumly to himself, "There are so many leaves on the ground. How will anyone ever notice me?" But he was wrong.

The children saw him and picked him up, and smiled. "Look at this beautiful leaf! It is the brightest leaf on the whole yard!" That made Leif a teeny tiny bit happy. But he *still* felt unimportant.

A gust of wind picked him up and carried him down the road, and under a bridge. There was a homeless man sitting on an old mattress. He looked very dirty and very tired. Leif thought to himself: "This is not a very nice place. There is garbage and leaves on the ground everywhere. How will anyone ever notice me here?" But he was wrong.

The homeless man looked up. He got off the mattress and walked over to Leif. "What a beautiful and bright leaf you are. Surely the brightest one I have ever seen." And Leif was just a teeny tiny bit happier. But he *still* felt insignificant.

The man threw Leif up into the sky and smiled as a gust of wind carried him down the road. He floated over a cemetery. Everyone looked very sad. Leif thought to himself, "I am just one leaf blowing in the wind today, how will anyone notice me?"

But he was wrong. Again.

A little girl looked up and pointed: "Look Mommy, look at the bright leaf!" Her mother looked up with tears in her eyes, and said, "What a beautiful leaf it is. The most beautiful leaf I have ever seen. It must have been sent down from heaven to give us a smile today." Leif was just a little happier than before. But he *still* felt small and unimportant.

He blew around a little longer and then continued on to a park. Children were playing in the leaves. "Look at how many leaves there are, surely no one will notice me here" thought Leif. Do you think he was right?

Of course not!

The children did play in the leaves, but one little boy pulled Leif from the pile. "Look how bright and beautiful this leaf is!" All the children came running. Leif was very happy. In fact, he was much happier than before. But, I am sure you can guess how he still felt.

Leif blew over many more fields, and the more big things he saw, the more small he felt. There were many people who told him how beautiful and bright he was, but every time he only felt happy for a little bit. Then he saw something bigger and felt insignificant again.

Finally, it was winter. Leif lay under a tree and watched as the snow sparkled and twinkled in the sun like a million tiny diamonds. I am sure you can guess how Leif felt.

As he lay there waiting, a little girl came along with her brother, and they sprinkled bird seed near the tree. Suddenly, the little girl saw Leif, and picked him up. "Look," she said to her brother, "This is the brightest leaf I have ever seen. I think I will take it home."

As the two walked back to their house, Leif looked around.

The house was very small. The rug inside the door had a hole in it. The curtains were dirty. In the corner, stood a small tree in a pot. It was not a big and tall tree, but a very small one, with only a few branches. It had a few nuts and some acorns hanging off its branches. Leif was confused. He thought that all Christmas trees were grand and tall. This one was certainly not.

The little girl took Leif and stuck him between the needles on a branch. Leif wasn't quite sure how he should feel right now.

"Look Mommy, I found something for our Christmas tree," she called excitedly. A thin woman came through the door and threw her hands up in the air.

"Sophie that is the most beautiful leaf I have ever seen! It is the most beautiful ornament on our Christmas tree!"

When Leif saw how excited they were, he felt excited too. Actually, he was more excited and happy than he ever had been.

He felt so happy, that he didn't feel unimportant or small at all. Can you guess how Leif felt?

Today was the happiest day of his life. For the first time he felt big. He felt important, and he felt proud that he had made this poor family so happy.

Today he realized that just because something is big, it is not always significant.

He realized that even though he was small, he was just as important as something bigger. He believed he was truly a significant leaf.

And he beamed with happiness, and looked brighter than he ever had before.

About the Author

My name is Elisabeth Tyndall. I am a primary-junior school teacher in my second year of supplying. I have had a passion for writing since I was a young girl, and have finally found the courage to publish my work. I have always had a vivid imagination, which I can credit to my brothers, with whom I would spend hours delving into the world of a place we called Happyville. I am married to a wonderful and supportive man, who was really the driving force to my publishing. Through all my doubt, he was my believer, and is always there helping me to reach as high as possible. He has taught me that even if you are tiny, you can accomplish great things and this first book is dedicated to him. We live on a small farm near Goderich, Ontario, with our cats, pigs, chickens, and a vast array of night crawlers.

LaVergne, TN USA
01 December 2010
206796LV00001B